Things I Know (And some things I wish I didn't)

Cleo Bell

India | USA | UK

Presentation by *BookLeaf Publishing*

Web: www.bookleafpub.com

E-mail: info@bookleafpub.com

ISBN: 9789358314830

First edition 2024

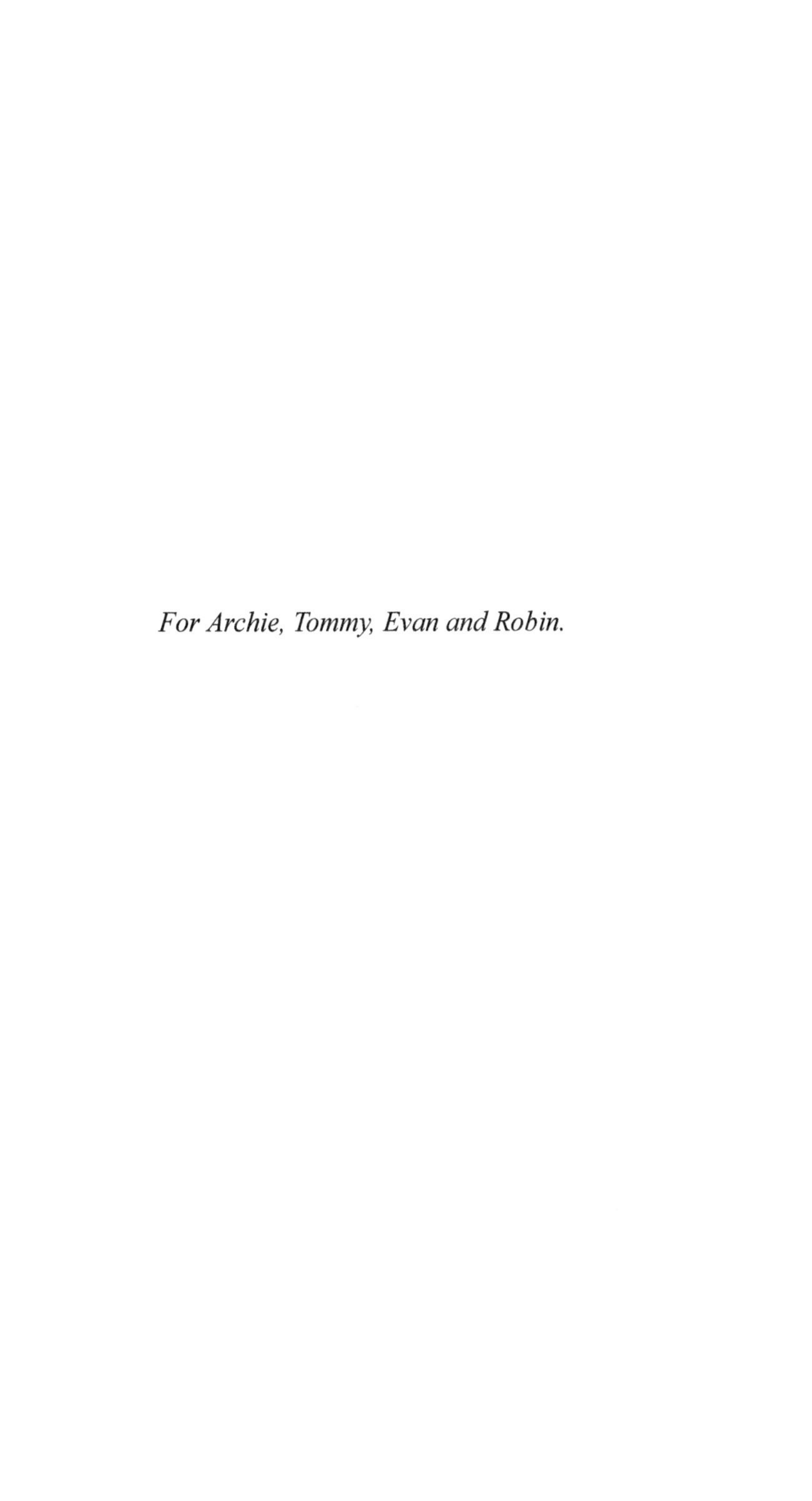

For Archie, Tommy, Evan and Robin.

ACKNOWLEDGEMENT

I would like to thank my family and friends for helping me to swim when I was drowning.

PREFACE

This collection of poems and ponderings is
about some of the most difficult times in my life.
Although the writing was hard, I also found it
therapeutic. I hope that you find something in
this book that helps you too.

I Wish

I wish I could take away your pain
Wrap it up
Collect it with magical threads
Bury it deep
Where it can't hurt anymore
To pull the strands from your body
Take them away
Lock them in a glass box
To see them from a safe distance.
I wish this wasn't true
And you could still be you.
A true original, they said.
They'll never be another
Remarkable, wonderful you
Who filled my life with love and light.
I want to see who you could be
If you had the chance to truly live
To make mistakes, to screw up
To change direction and start again.
I wish I could take it away
Give you the life being stolen from you
I wish ...
I wish ...
But wishes don't always come true.

Other

There are words to describe people
Who have lost the ones they love
Orphan,
Widow,
Widower
But there are no words for a mother
Without her child
A childless mother?
A mother without a child?
Or are you always a mother?
Or perhaps something other?
Maybe there is no word
Because some things can not be named.

The Living Dead

How can I feel this grief for you when you are
still here?
I want to make the most of you
To make you happy and overflow with delight
To inhale you
Store you in memory deep within my soul
To take out on rainy days
Or sunny days
Or any days
When you are not here.
I want to bottle you
To preserve you
To freeze us both in time
Back when everything was ok
When we didn't see this coming
Didn't know it was true.
I want everything to stop
So we can stay here
You and I forever
While everything else moves on around us
But we can't
Because one day soon you will stop
And I will still be here
Living the days you couldn't
Moving forward with the world

Trying desperately to bring you with me
Because I don't know how to be
If I can't be with you.

Happy

You were there
That is all I remember
It is all I need to know.

How to Love a Wild One

There are some who can not be tamed
They need to run wild and free
To live on their own terms
Experiencing all that the world can be
If you cage them
They will become less
No longer who they are
Half a person
A life half lived
A bright light dimmed
To cast a long shadow
Of roads not taken
Promise unfulfilled
Regrets for the unknown.
The only way to love a wild one
Is to let them go
Out to experience all of life's joys and pitfalls
Excitements and roadblocks
To be who they are truly meant to be
You can not cage a wild heart
But if you set them free
They will love you with the power
Of everything they were meant to be.

Second Chances

I thought I had my chance at love
Met the one and took our shot
But time and age and normal life
Turned us into something else
Love making way for indifference and apathy
The remnants of a friendship still intact.

I wasn't looking for love
I thought that it had passed me by
Instead I was looking for adventure
And funny stories to tell my friends
The whole Internet my playground
With people I wouldn't otherwise meet.

The muscly man from far away
The one with bad intentions
The unsolicited pictures
The older one who just wanted friendship
And to remove me from my clothes
The sweet one who was grieving.

The one I really liked
Who cancelled on me very late
Saying he wasn't ready
Code for: I just don't like you that much.

You came up repeatedly
I discounted you right from the start
Not what I was looking for
Then a message
So different from the rest
It made me laugh out loud.

A first meeting under a clock
The feeling of always knowing you
I didn't expect to feel this way
Just like I did when I was young
A rush of emotions and giddiness
Distracted thoughts and daydreams.

I don't believe in second chances
But maybe that's why you were there
To remind me
That life can always surprise.

Speak No Ill

They say you should not speak ill of the dead
But what is the harm?
The dead can not hear
They don't care what we say
Or don't say
Or do
Or don't do
They can not hurt
They should say speak no ill of the living
They hear your words
They hurt.

Mundane

I imagined I sat down to dinner
With my children yesterday
We talked about their day
I had to persuade them to eat
All of the food that I made
Nothing extraordinary
Something that happens so often it is rushed
Taken for granted
A chore
Something to be done until the next thing can be
done
Except it isn't
Because I never got to eat with my children.

Who Are You?

Everybody always wanted me to be someone
Who they thought I was
The good girl
The fun girl
The sinner
The saint
The boring one
The dream one
The sensible one
The beautiful one
The dumb one
Everyone always wanted me to be someone
Except who I was.

Hungry?

We sit in the kitchen together
You with the appetite that once could never be
filled
I present you with things
Stroke your soft head
Tell you it's delicious
Anything to get you to eat something
Strength goes in at the mouth
My Grandmother used to say
I look at you so small and frail
Somehow less than what you once were
But still with a spirit so strong
A sparkle in your eye
An unwillingness to be defeated
I push the food towards you
It's good, I say
You eye it suspiciously
Then lick your lips
My heart expand as you begin
You know you need to eat
However much you don't want to
You look at me with appreciative eyes
As I turn the plate
Present you with the tastiest food
And you eat

I release the breath that I was holding
Strength goes in at the mouth.

Love

We sit for the longest time
You and I
Together in our silence
As I gently try to persuade you
To do the things to keep you here
I want to let you go
But I don't want you to leave
Tears roll silently down my face
And I'm ashamed
For grieving you
When you're beside me
We sit together you and I
As I persuade you
One more breath
One more bite
Your eyes on mine so full of love
Together in our misery
We sit together you and I
It's the price we pay
For our love.

The Unknown

The worst kind of disasters
Are the ones we don't see coming
The earthquake
The unexpected heartbreak
The nothing to one hundred miles an hour
The oncoming train that no one can stop
The young and perfectly healthy
Reassuringly ordinary
Until it isn't.

Old Age

To be old is a privilege
That we forget
Among the wrinkles and aches and pains
The battle scars and lessons learned
And unfamiliar symphony now created when
moving from your chair

To be old is to have lived
To see things change
To complain how things are not as good as they
were
When statistically it always gets better
We do not live in statistics
But in the way we feel.

To be old is to have chances
To love, to care, to cry, to yearn
To have your heart broken
And pick yourself up and try again

We don't value the old
Until we realise the privilege it is
The only thing I ever wish for my children now
Is that they will be old.

Ordinary

I wish for you an ordinary life
Of Friday night movies
And Saturday afternoon football matches
A job you like, most of the time
A boss you love, but sometimes loathe
I wish you birthday meals
And holidays
To places the sun warms your skin
I wish you love
That's not dramatic
A steady love, dependable
No earthquakes and tsunamis
I wish for you an unextraordinary life
Where nothing really happens
But that means everything happens
Just as you would expect
I wish for you an ordinary life
I wish for you a life.

Try IVF

Try IVF, they said
It works, I know this person who ...
And I forget the rest
Try IVF, they said
Wrap all your dreams and love and hope in it
This option is the best
I remember the extreme gratitude
The privilege felt to take this path
The tremendous joy of a second round
That didn't leave me ill for weeks
The beauty of knowing before I was told
Because some things you just know.
My exclamation at the ease
The counsellors wise words
'No one but you would think this easy,
because your path has been so hard'

Try IVF , they said
As the pure joy of nausea made me elated
The trickle of hope growing into a stream
From a tiny heartbeat on a screen.
IVF is hard, they said
Even when you win
It leaves you broken
With battle scars invisible to the naked eye

With levels like that a 90% chance of success
As the stream of hope became Niagara Falls
Hurtling towards the 12 week scan
The nausea and headaches
Lulling a false sense of safety.

I just need a minute, she said
My colleagues help to have a look
'What does that mean?' he asked
As I responded, 'nothing good'
You shouldn't be here, she said
No heartbeat pumping on the screen
The bluntness of her lack of care
Somehow causing more pain
Than the whole world collapsing around me

Very common, they said
Just unlucky
You can always try again
This flower is here
To help you with the unthinkable
The unimaginable
As if somehow a well intentioned crochet flower
Could put back together broken pieces
And restart two hearts.

Me

I don't know who I am anymore
I don't know who to be
If you're not here to be you anymore
Then how can I be me?

Euthanasia

Today I murdered my best friend
It's not the first time either
Does this make me a mass murderer?
A serial killer?
Even though I didn't administer the final blow?
It was the right thing, a kindness they say
You had nothing left
Except days of misery
Pain and suffering
To slip away, no longer you
Unable to really move or be
I wish you could tell me what you want
The right thing to do
Then I wouldn't have to live
With the guilt of my decision
But I know that you are telling me
By the way you are sleeping
The way you can't eat
The look in your eye
The stillness in your body
You will always be
My hardest goodbye.

Cleaning

The wonderful thing about cleaning
Is that you can take something grimy, dirty and
broken
And with the right tools
And a little hard work
You can make it look completely new again
Like it was never covered in grease and grime
Never looked anything other than its best
The past completely disappears
And can not haunt it any more
The wonderful thing about cleaning
Is you can take something old and battered
And restore it to it's very best
All it takes is a little effort
If only it was the same for people.

Grief

There are a thousand ways to grieve
Not one of them is wrong
You could sit and cry for days
Or put it in a song
For me, I must keep busy
And put my hands to work
To keep the feelings inside me
Would make me go berserk
So I must keep on moving
And doing to distract
For when it finally catches me
They'll be no going back.

A Wish for the New Year

This year I've decided a new little test
Of something to do to see if it's for the best
I've decided to put myself first
I mean what could happen?
What could be the worst?
Instead of putting others needs before me
I'll fix myself first
And see how that'll be
It seems to be what others do
Would it be so bad if I did it too?
It doesn't mean I'll become selfish
And only do the things I wish
It just means that I'll be a priority too
In all the things I decide to do
I mean really would the world fall apart?
If I looked after myself
And followed my heart
So this year I will start to say no
To going to places I don't want to go
And I'll try to make sure that when I say yes
It's to things that I love
That will not cause me stress.

Tomorrow

The wonderful thing about tomorrow
Is that it is always there waiting
Full of possibility

The heart breaking thing about tomorrow
Is that sometimes
There isn't one.

www.ingramcontent.com/pod-product-compliance
Lightning Source LLC
LaVergne TN
LVHW021344200726
843509LV00014B/2660